Trust and Transformative Technologies

A Public Relations Essay

David Phillips FCIPR FSNCR

TRUST AND TRANSFORMATIVE TECHNOLOGIES

Copyright © 2012 David Phillips
All rights reserved.
ISBN:10:1727269713
ISBN-13:9781727269710

Transformative Technologies Essays

About these essays

The Transformative Technologies Public Relations essays are designed to provide perspectives on the practice and theory of Public Relations in the early 21st century.

They examine technology developments as they may affect practice in the current or near future and point towards areas of research, development education and deployment that the industry needs to consider.

The evolution of PR practice when the key tools were listening and oratory; press monitoring and media releases to social media monitoring and interventions are part of a rich and continuing range of practices.

However, we have gone past these approaches to affecting relationships. Deep Learning using masses of data available from online interaction via the Internet, Internet of Things and newer capabilities such as Bluetooth Mesh is the new information environment.

It is awesome in the detailed information generated, transmitted, monitored and processed.

To imagine that one can have a map of an organisation's existence identified as a Stakeholder Group, is no longer adequate when minute by minute there is a capability to discover the extent to which an individual is a stakeholder is with associates and has other interests. There is free software to define mood and location and much much more. We have gone beyond Online Public Relations.

Here I hope to introduce the technologies as they affect big Public Relations issues.

About the Author

The technology interventions in professional life and, notably, Public Relations has become something of a hobby and hence these essays.

It all began when I started to use computerisation for media evaluation in the late 1970's (when I wrote the Kogan Page book 'Evaluating Press Coverage). Later, in the 1990's I wrote books on internet moderated PR (notably Online Public Relations, Kogan Page) and I have not stopped since.

These essays are my perspective after a career covering political organisation (local, Parliamentary and European election management), corporate affairs (Lancer Boss Group), PR evaluation (Founded Media Measurement), press relations (Phillips and Company) and corporate digital consultancy (including a Central Bank). I have published five text books for the PR sector, lectured at five universities and spoken at conferences on four continents. I am well published in academic journals on PR subjects and continue to lecture part time in Lisbon and UK universities.

I am a Fellow of the Chartered Institute of Public Relations.

Now, in my, so called, retirement, I pursue what is changing my erstwhile profession.

While the subject of these essays seem to be at random, they reflect some of the concerns that people in PR raise from time to time and where I have some expertise or specialist knowledge.

1 what is Public Relations

Today, there is a debate as to the nature and role of public relations. Is it really a communication discipline or is it something else is one such topic. To write these essays I have taken a particular view.

My view is that PR is a profession that plans and executes changes in relationships and thereby wealth. If PR is an empire, then communications is, to my mind the 'regulus' of PR. Regulus is Latin for a 'petty king' . Undoubtedly communication is a key and important element in changing relationships and value but there is a greater purpose in Public Relations.

In the paper "Cultural Relations Theory" my colleague Dr Anne Danbury and I (Danbry and Phillips 2018) describe an evolution of PR in which big data extracted from online content, social media and the Internet of Things (IoT) interaction provides the resource to identify cultures large and small and their inter-relationships.

Historic influencer segmentation such as Publics (Grunig 1997), Stakeholders (Freeman 1984)[1] etc. are seen to be inadequate in an era of artificial intelligence.

In the Culture Relations Theory, we posit that "modern technologies detect and process micro values to expose intercultural nuance which is now a potential tool for relationship management'. A large part of relationship building and management involves trust as an intangible asset.

This intangible asset concept is eloquently discussed by Professor Gregory and Dr Jon White in a CIPR podcast (Gregory and White, 2018). It is a tantalising idea that very soon we will be able to audit trust in tangible terms sufficiently robust for inclusion on a balance sheet.

The question is, whether this theory and these new technologies have a role to play in isolating the elements of trust in an attempt to be able to identify levers of management that aid development of commercially valuable 'trust'.

It is from this perspective of PR that these essays are written.

---

[1] Freeman, R. (1984). Strategic management. Boston: Pitman.

2 WHO SAYS TRUST IS IMPORTANT

Trust is a subject of much debate

It has risen in prominence in recent years as those institutions that depend on trust have failed.

Relationships can work with remarkably low levels of trust as long as both people and organisations have a common objective. However, the effectiveness of the relationship will definitely improve as trust builds.

High levels of trust speeds up decisions and business processes and consequently lowers costs. As the level of trust goes down, the speed of doing business goes down and costs go up.

When distrust exists, relationships and communications are ineffective and everything has to be proved or validated..

Most of the cost associated with measuring and checking performance, writing complex and detailed contracts and meeting with people is associated with the lack of trust.

Where trust exists, where you can rely on the other person to be truthful, all that is needed to manage most work is a brief communication to ensure understanding and a 'hand shake'; real or virtual. Trust is a key element in relationship management.

Evidence of poor management shakes confidence and has a cost.

Jamie Nimmo writing in the Mail on Sunday on 25 August 2018 revealed that Britain's biggest banks paid out £71 billion for misconduct in the decade since the financial crisis of 2008.

The staggering costs for Royal Bank of Scotland, Lloyds Banking Group, Barclays and HSBC stem from fines, legal fees and compensation for mistreated customers. There is a way of measuring this hit on trust in banking. £71 billion is £1000 per person in the UK. The share value of the UK banking sector dropped 10% in the last six month of 2017 (https://shareprices.com/sectors/banks).

A 2018 PWC report based on opinion research highlights trust as a key issue. It notes "The financial services industry's traditional response to concern about consumer mistrust has been to stress goals such as greater transparency and improved financial education. However, ...further work of this type might be relatively limited, at least in isolation. Though greater transparency is the single improvement most likely to rebuild consumer trust in financial services, even here fewer than one in two people (46%) would be impressed by such changes."

So it is no surprise that Sir David Walker, (Barclays Bank Chairman) at the Federal Reserve Bank of New York workshop on reforming culture and behaviours in the financial services industry, put trust at the top of his concerns.

"I am grateful", he said, "to the philosopher Onora O'Neill for reference to very relevant advice from Confucius that three things are needed for government: weapons, food and trust:

"If a ruler cannot hold on to all three, he should give up the weapons first and the food next.

"Trust should be guarded to the end. Without trust we cannot stand".

Sir David continued: "It is not only rulers and governments who prize and need trust. Each of us, and every profession and every institution needs trust. We need it because we have to be able to rely on others acting as they say that they will and because we need others to accept that we will act as we say we will - in other words that they and we ourselves are trustworthy."

Warren Buffet, the American businessman, investor, philanthropist and CEO of Berkshire Hathaway understands the importance of corporate culture and adhering to a code of ethics. He has been quoted saying:
"Lose money and I will forgive you. Lose even a shred of reputation and I will be ruthless. Wealth can always be recreated, but reputation takes a lifetime to build and often only a moment to destroy."

Trust in government is likewise, the subject of much debate.

Lara Fleischer, of the Organisation for Economic Co-operation and Development (OECD) Statistics Directorate discussed trust in governments during 2017. Her introduction is informative:

"Is trust between people and their governments crumbling? What the great philosopher Jean-Jacques Rousseau called the social contract, whereby free citizens voluntarily agree to concede authority to the state in their own interest, could be in question.

"The OECD's 'How's Life? 2017' report finds that only 38% of people in OECD countries say they trust their government. In 2006, this figure was around 42%.

Why is there such a "disconnect" between citizens and their elected representatives?"

The 2018 Edelman Trust Barometer (https://www.edelman.com//trust-barometer) revealed "a world of seemingly stagnant distrust. People's trust in business, government, NGOs and media remained largely unchanged from 2017 — 20 of 28 markets surveyed now lie in distruster territory, up one from last year."

Brands, too, have a problem:

In a September 2017 article, Katie Richards at AdWeek reports:

"At American Express, fighting to win back consumers' trust in a world of data breaches and fake news isn't advertising. Elizabeth Rutledge at American Express said the brand relies a lot on word of mouth to spread positive messages.

"It's the best way for us to show our brand authentically through other customers who have stories to share about the experience they've had," Rutledge said. "That's better than any ad in terms of a reference point.

"For Publicis Groupe's chief growth officer Rishad Tobaccowala, it's less about advertising and creative and more about marketing and product innovation.

"In many cases you may want to cut your advertising budget to improve your product or service."

Another key priority for Tobaccowala is earning back clients' trust by first addressing two issues.

"One is what are you doing with my money? And the harder question is are you relevant to me anymore?" he said. "We have to be open about what we are doing to change."

At PayPal, it's about putting the consumer at the center of everything and building trust over time.

"Part of what tech companies can do is to help our customers connect with each other as well as connect with us," said Franz Paasche, SVP, corporate affairs and communications at PayPal. "I think it's an evolutionary process where we are learning from our customers, and they are learning from us."

Amazon takes a similar approach to PayPal, especially when it comes to creative work.

"The essence of any great brief starts with the customer, and the essence of an awful brief is that it starts with business," Amazon executive creative director Michael Boychuk said.

It seems there is a need for all walks of life to understand the nature of trust, its significance and how to manage it.

Trust is a key element of relationships and thus is a core part of public relations. With trust comes a more profound relationship and the value of the relationship is tangible in many ways, not the least in its ability to lubricate trade, commerce and government.

But what of trust in this era of transformative technologies?

3 ABOUT TRUST, THE QUESTIONS

When we become more specific and attempt to understand the effects of technologies on trust, the debate becomes quite interesting.

For example: can the emerging technologies scrape, analyse and isolate the elements of trust?

Are there new technologies that can be used as a substitute for trust?
Is more transparency, at a time when people's lives and institutions are more exposed the answer?

Is evidence in people's public lives sufficient to identify levers of management that aid development of commercially valuable 'trust'? Alternatively, is trust a key element in the value of publics, stakeholders or cultures?

By no means is trust in a PR context likely to be subsumed by computers, but we find, the practical application of technologies will add weight to the academic and professional discourse on the importance of trust in public relations.

There are so many questions.

4 ABOUT TRUST, THE QUESTIONS

There are a number of definitions of trust. Perhaps one might examine them with transformative technologies in mind.

Trust is the assured reliance on the character, ability, strength, or truth of someone or something: one in which confidence is placed, suggests Merriam Webster Dictionary.

Here technology can help. Someone or something can be identified either because the practitioner knows what it is (such as a client, company, government etc) or, alternatively, because the entity has become obvious using the network analysis techniques detailed by distinguished academics such as John Scott and Mark Newman.

Network analysis is very good at identifying entities from Big Data generated by Google, Facebook, Pinterest etc. This sort of process can identify cultures, organisations and communities using software like IBM's Watson.

By using analysis of attributes associated with such entities it is now possible to assess relative characteristics, abilities, strengths and truths as between one entity and another.

Another definition of trust is "Dependence on something future or contingent: hope".

Once again, we have some capability to identify dependencies by using network analysis and or artificial intelligence.

Mark Newman shows us how dependant one entity is on another in his Complex Systems Advanced Academic Workshop lecture (see below).

A methodology for testing dependence on elements of entities will show the extent of vulnerability the organisation is to a range of changes (this is advanced stuff and is, but possible, serious relationship management).

Alternatively some AI programmes working on sequential data will predict (and offer a measure of confidence in such a prediction) the extent to which the next event is true and by how much.

It is not dissimilar to the AI models that drive weather forecasts. Here is the prospect to allow us to evaluate how much we can trust a relationships' future stability.

"Reliance on future payment for property (such as merchandise) delivered i.e. credit" is a further definition of trust. Can I trust this person, company (bank?), organisation or government to pay up?

Here, we might look at a mobile example used to predict trust in creditworthiness.

In November 2015, Roxanne Bauer reported in the World Bank blog how Bjorkegren and Grissen were able to predict who among the sampled individuals would repay their bank loan (http://bit.ly/2PiYSFN).

The insight was based on how the individuals used their mobile phones before applying for the loan.

In fact, the predictive accuracy of their method approaches that of credit scoring methods using traditional data. Individuals in the highest quartile of risk were 6 times more likely to default than those in the lowest quartile.

Armed with this knowledge, the bank that participated in this study could eliminate 43% of their defaults by eliminating the 25% of people who are most risky. The 75% of borrowers who are likely to repay the loans would not be affected.

We learn from this that there are a wide range of technologies available to PR managers as mobile takes centre stage in this example. One can continue to explore more definitions of Trust and seek out the technology solutions that help to define, measure, predict or manage trustworthiness.

What these example are telling us is that there is considerable value in using such technologies available to the Public Relations Profession.

Further, understanding of trust is its key and fundamental part of being a balanced human being.

According to Erik Erikson, we all encounter a certain crisis that contributes to our psychosocial growth at each of his stages of psychosocial development. Trust, he says is an early essential in psychological development.[2]

---

[2] https://www.psychologynotesha.com/erikerikson/

The first part of the Erikson stages starts from infant to about 18 months.

At this stage, infants must learn how to trust others, particularly those who care for their basic needs. They should feel that they are being cared for and that all their needs are met.

Small babies are new to this world and may view the outside world as threatening. Depending on how they are treated by people around them, the sense of threat can be replaced by trust.

When this happens, they gain a sense of security and begin to learn to trust people around them.

Trust is analysed at an interpersonal level by academics like Jeffrey A Simpson[4] and Julian B Rotter[5]. They discuss the positive and potential negative consequences of being high or low in interpersonal trust in current social life, particularly in interacting with ordinary people.

A summary and analysis of previous investigations led Rotter to the following conclusions:

"People who trust more are less likely to lie and are possibly less likely to cheat or steal. They are more likely to give others a second chance and to respect the rights of others. The high truster is less likely to be unhappy, conflicted, or maladjusted, and is liked more and sought out as a friend more often, by both low-trusting and high-trusting others."

"When gullibility is defined as naiveté or foolishness and trust is defined as believing others in the absence of clear-cut reasons to disbelieve, then it can be shown over a series of studies that high trusters are not more gullible than low trusters[6].

Research by Garske[7], indicated 'trust tended to be related with personality traits that suggested a social orientation and adaptive functioning'.

Trust was also viewed as bearing a relationship with concrete thinking and conformity. Correlations between the factors of the Interpersonal Trust Scale (Political Trust, Paternal Trust, and Trust of Strangers) were similar to the above correlations but less substantial. The total trust score appeared to be a better predictor of personality than any of its factor scores."[8]

In short, trust is a fundamental human driver. It is a contract between persons and or institutions in which the one undertakes to warrant values and capabilities to a given and transparent extent.

It is a socially shared phenomenon.

Trust can be developed at a point in time where there is rudimentary mutual recognition between people, organisations and cultures and other entities such as governments and the body politic.

It is a key component of relationships.

Trust can be a one, or two-way exchange or formed via a cultural network. It is expressed by people and cultures in tokens exchanged with one or more other cultures. Such tokens can be both tangible and intangible. Personal cultures of trusting people have some very significant benefits.

This means that there is no possibility of relationships being formed without at least some element of positive or negative trust between the parties.

There is an element of timeliness in trust. It can form, change and develop between parties over time. It is to a greater or lesser degree, durable.

The extent to which there is greater or lesser trust as between one organisation and another, or expressed another way, between one culture and another is also an element in the trust equation.

Finally, the extent to which values are acceptable, namely, are regarded as positive, negative or emotionally empathetic as part of the culture of the organisation is important.

Trust is evident in person to person and social as well as commercial relationships. As such the elements associated with positive and negative trust can be identified and monitored by transformative technologies. Such intelligence can then be processed to aid Trust management.

Thus, trust, the key element of relationships is at the core of all Public Relations if the profession chooses to deploy technological solutions. Could such capability be good enough to prevent wars? I believe so but not without much research. Nevertheless, a great prize.

5 IS TRUST VALUABLE?

The extent to which trust is valuable will, no doubt, affect how much PR practice invests in its management.

There are many current case studies where we see the evaporation of trust in corporate values in corporately cataclysmic terms.

Facebook, Oxfam, Grenfell Tower and Bell Pottinger are cases where trust in values, competencies and culture have contributed to loss of confidence, disastrous financial performance and survival.

Trust is an element of corporate survival. It forms the basis upon which organisations can trade. It has wide implications.

During the 2008–2009 financial crisis, firms with high social capital, as measured by corporate social responsibility (CSR) intensity, had stock returns that were four to seven percentage points higher than firms with low social capital. High-CSR firms also experienced higher profitability, growth, and sales per employee relative to low-CSR firms, and they raised more debt.

This evidence suggests that the trust between a firm and both its stakeholders and investors, built through investments in social capital, pays off when the overall level of trust in corporations and markets suffers a negative shock (Lins et al 2017[3]).

Trust is positively linked with share price volatility (Audi, Loughran and McDonald 2016[4]).

Research has revealed that relationships between third parties and employees has trust value. For example, a salesperson's ethical behaviour leads to higher customer satisfaction trust and loyalty to banks that the salesperson represents (Roman S 2012).

Professor Peter Corning puts it this way: "In fact, smoothly-operating markets depend on trust. Another way of looking at a complex modern economy is that it represents a vast network of cooperation and mutually beneficial exchanges of goods and services. And trust is the lubricant that makes it all work."

The Edelman 'Trust Barometer', said to be representative of 84% of the global population, posits that "As we begin 2018, we find the world in a new phase in the loss of trust: the unwillingness to believe information, even from those closest to us. The loss of confidence in information channels and sources is the fourth wave of the trust tsunami. The moorings of institutions have already been dangerously undermined by the three previous waves: fear of job loss due to globalization and automation; the Great Recession, which created a crisis of confidence in traditional authority figures and institutions while undermining the

---

3 LINS, K., SERVAES, H. and TAMAYO, A. (2017). Social Capital, Trust, and Firm Performance: The Value of Corporate Social Responsibility during the Financial Crisis. *The Journal of Finance*, 72(4), pp.1785-1824.

4 Connelly, B., Crook, T., Combs, J., Ketchen, D. and Aguinis, H. (2015). Competence- and Integrity-Based Trust in Interorganizational Relationships: Which Matters More?. Journal of Management, 44(3), pp.919-945.

middle class; and the effects of massive global migration. Now, in this fourth wave, we have a world without common facts and objective truth, weakening trust even as the global economy recovers."[9]

News and sources of information are key drivers in trust as both the Edelman and Ipsos Mori Veracity Index[5] surveys show.

Trust has a role in macro relationships across the globe.

The cost of developing a trusting relationship can be high. Creating a contract between a new supplier and an organization will involve the cost of references and data exchange and much more in the selling/buying decision. Second time round, these costs are much reduced and over a long period of time may virtually vanish. Such relationships are lubricated by the implied trust.

The World Economic Forum notes the massive and cost implications of failure of trust:

"If a contract fails to allocate responsibilities adequately, incentives to breach obligations and create disputes can arise. Increasingly, larger capital projects and a lack of trust between parties are leading to ever more complex contracts that are hard to understand."

It would seem from the above that identifying the elements of trust is a big job and sorting out all the elements to provide a practical management structure is hard."[6]

Global accountants Price Waterhouse Coopers note:

---

[5] http://bit.ly/2F6SEXW
[6] . http://bit.ly/2ES2spE

"Trust is even more important where you rely upon others to keep your promises. Specialisation, offshoring, outsourcing and cost cutting – this is the reality of business and your reliance on third parties will only grow.

"A complex portfolio of relationships needs to work effectively to deliver the promises you make to all your stakeholders."[7]

How, for example, can the PR practitioners identify the extent to which one organisation is more trustworthy than others? How can we change levels of trust between cultures?

The extent to which an organisation's cultural values are stable or are warranted internally or by external agents are elements of trust. A culture of openness might be valuable when manifest as trust in commercial relationships.

But, what about online trust and its value?

A study by Eric W.K. See-To, and Kevin K.W. Ho, use the theories in trust and value co-creation to analyze how electronic Word-of-Mouth (eWOM) affects purchase intention in social network sites (SNSs). In particular, they developed a theoretical model to study how a range of factors interact with each other and note that eWOM has a direct impact on purchase intention, and has an indirect impact on purchase intention which is moderated by consumers' trust on the underlying product. eWOM also has an impact on value co-creation, and value co-creation has an effect on purchase intention.

Consumers' trust on a product has an impact on value co-creation, and the message source in the SNSs moderates the impacts of eWOM on

---

[7] https://pwc.to/2F3m61j

consumers' trust on a product, value co-creation, and purchase intention.

Trust online has a commercial value too.

What we discover is that there is a lot of research into the value of trust.

The online part of trust is important. In many research papers there are good and solid approaches and some leading figures such as Professor Jie Wu at the Department of Computer and Information Sciences, Temple University, Philadelphia offers a range of robust approaches.

What we have found is that no one approach fits all but that is not the end of the story. There are many people seeking methods for measuring trust and, in doing so, are beginning to value trust in many instances.

6 THE ONLINE NETWORK - A GOLDEN RESOURCE

In his paper for the Chartered Institute of Public Relations "Humans Still Needed - An analysis of skills and tools in Public Relations", Jean Valin writes: "Fundamental human traits such as empathy, trust, humour and relationship building can't be automated – at least not yet." (Valin, 2018)[8].

Against this claim we can examine the extent to which emerging and transformative technologies had already met, or superseded Valin's claim that trust cannot be automated.

The development of technologies is very rapid.

Rana el Kaliouby is the CEO and cofounder of Affectiva. Writing in MIT Review she asks "What if, instead of smart speakers (Google/Alexa), autonomous vehicles, television sets, connected refrigerators, mobile phones—were aware of your emotions? What if they sensed nonverbal behavior in real time?

"Mood-aware technologies would make personalized recommendations and encourage people to do things differently, better, or faster.

---

[8] https://www.cipr.co.uk/sites/default/files/11497_CIPR_AIinPR_A4_v7.pdf

"Today," she says, "an emerging category of AI—artificial emotional intelligence, or emotion AI—is focused on developing algorithms that can identify not only basic human emotions such as happiness, sadness, and anger but also more complex cognitive states such as fatigue, attention, interest, confusion, distraction, and more."

Indeed, IBM's Watson AI capability already has free off-the-shelf modules to assess emotions, mood and attitude.

In his book Heart of the Machine: Our Future in a World of Artificial Emotional Intelligence, Richard Yonck[9] says " artificial emotional intelligence, or Emotion AI is rapidly being incorporated into everything from market research testing to automotive interfaces to chatbots and social robotics, this is a branch of AI that will continue to rapidly grow over the next few decades. "

Network theory and in particular the work of Professor John Scott (his is a very important book: Social Network Analysis Sage 2017) and work on on community and spectra by Prof. Mark Newman helps us too (I commend his lecture to the Complex Systems Advanced Academic Workshop at the College of Literature, Science, and the Arts at the University of Michigan
https://www.youtube.com/watch?v=JERIwTzIzmA and his book 'Networks' - second edition is a key publications).

These prominent academics hand us a ready made ability to use digital data from web search, and mobile location as well as the words used on mobile, laptop and fixed computers and, more recently, IoT devices including the Google Assistant or Alexa on your coffee table (OK, I

---

[9] Yonck, R. (2017) <u>Heart of the Machine: Our Future in a World of Artificial Emotional Intelligence</u>. Arcade Publishing, NY.

know, there are ethical issues here - but that is another Transformative Technologies essay!).

Using this well established academic work (and visualisation tools such as these in KDnuggets (http://bit.ly/2PlzIGy) we can use a range of data now readily available as API's (Application Programming Interface) from vendors such a Google, Bing, Facebook Twitter etc.

The time, location, person, technology, channel, content, interaction and many more attributes of modern communication has become the raw material for network analysis for PR.

It is already mined and forged into cultural models describing elements in relationships among a wide range of other analysis.

Its adoption by the PR profession is important.

The ability to identify networks of people, of institutions, ideas, mood, attitudes as well as opinion formers and disruptors is thereby available to the practitioner.

Organisational values and the penumbra of associated values describe and prescribe the culture of the organisation.

Many such values explicitly or implicitly represent trust (mood, attitude and relationships can be data combined to identify relative trust as between cultures and organisations).

Put bluntly, there is the potential capability to use this mine of information to identify those elements that measure trust and the trustworthiness of organisations, people and institutions.

... and then use such capability for good or ill?

Should we do it? Is this too far?

Will others (perhaps less ethical or as rouge driven as Bell Pottinger or a dangerous government) develop such capabilities?

Meanime, the nature of Public Relations is changing.

In the paper "Cultural Relations Theory" we describe an evolution of PR in which big data extracted from online content, social media and the Internet of Things (IoT) interaction provides the resource to identify cultures large and small and their inter-relationships[10].

Historic influencer segmentation such as Publics[11] (Grunig 1997), Stakeholders (Freeman 1984)[12] etc. are seen to be inadequate in an era of Big Data, Deep Learning and artificial intelligence.

A large part of relationship building and management involves trust as an intangible asset.

---

[10] Danbury A and Phillips David GH "Cultural Relations Theory - an evolution powered by Transformative Technologies" Presented to the 23rd International Conference on Corporate and Marketing Communications Exeter April 2018

[11] Grunig, J. E. (1997). A situational theory of publics: Conceptual history, recent challenges and new research. In D. Moss, T. MacManus & D. Veri (Eds.), Public relations research: An international perspective (pp. 3–46). London: International Thomson Business.

[12] Freeman, R. (1984). Strategic management. Boston: Pitman.

This intangible asset concept is eloquently discussed by Professor Gregory and Dr Jon White in a CIPR podcast[13] (Gregory and White, 2018).

It is a tantalising idea that very soon we will be able to audit trust in tangible terms sufficiently robust for inclusion on a balance sheet.

Can this theory and these new technologies have a role to play in isolating the elements of trust in an attempt to be able to identify levers of management that aid development of commercially valuable 'trust'?

Meanwhile, there is a case for supporting Valin's view.

At a recent AI conference, MIT brain and cognitive sciences professor Josh Tenenbaum explained his views on the difference between our present state of AI and the long-term quest for human levels of intelligence.

Human-level intelligence requires the ability to go beyond data and machine learning algorithms. Humans are able to build models of the world as they perceive it, including practical, everyday common sense knowledge, and then use these models to explain their actions and decisions.

According to Prof. Tenenbaum, three-month-old babies have a more common sense understanding of the world around them than any AI application ever built. An AI application starts with a blank slate before

---

[13] 6. Gregory, P. and White, D. (2018). Platinum Podcast Show 2: PR as a strategic management function. [online] SoundCloud. Available at:
https://soundcloud.com/cipr_uk/platinum-podcast-show-2-pr-as-a-strategic-management-function [Accessed 25 Jul. 2018].

learning from patterns in the data it analyzes, while babies start off with a genetic head start and a brain structure that allows them to learn much more than data and patterns.

However, there is the ability to evolve technologies (as I speculate above) to 'automate' the nature of levels of trust as between organisations and relevant communities/cultures.

This is not as fanciful as some may imagine. One such technology is found in the use and application of BlockChains. From this one may infer that there already exists a computer substitute for financial transactions that is beyond the frailties of of interbank trading and the need for central clearing banks.

In this paper, I postulate the Blockchain development is but a first step.

7 TECHNOLOGY SUBSTITUTES FOR TRUST

IBM has developed a blockchain to verify the jewellery supply chain[14].

Called TrustChain, Its capability is such that a consumer is able to use a smartphone and scan a QR code on the diamond and see a visual of the entire supply chain.

Led by authors such as Don Tapscott, the nature of Blockchain as a computer programme that enforces trust is important. The Open University puts is very well:

"Blockchain is most commonly known as the technology underpinning the Bitcoin cryptocurrency. But in recent years the open source code of the Bitcoin, blockchain has been taken and extended by many groups to expand its capabilities. Blockchain technology, which can be thought of as a public distributed ledger, promises to revolutionise the financial world. "

Basically Blockchain is used to transfer information from one computer to another absolutely securely. Only the sender and receiver have access

---

[14] **IBM TrustChain**
https://techcrunch.com/2018/04/26/ibm-introduces-trustchain-a-blockchain-to-verify-the-jewelry-supply-chain/

to the data. Blockchain cannot be hacked or sent to the wrong person. We can trust it as a technology in many applications.

A World Economic Forum survey in 2015 found that those polled believe that there will be a tipping point for the government use of blockchain [20] by 2023[21]. Governments, large banks, software vendors and companies involved in stock exchanges (especially the Nasdaq stock exchange) are investing heavily in the area.

For example, the UK Government recently announced that it is investing £10M into blockchain research and Santander have identified 20-25 internal use cases for the technology and predict a reduction of banks' infrastructure costs by up to £12.8 billion a year [22].

So much for the future. Now we are beginning to see real deployment of blockchain.

Civil, is an example. It is a two-year-old crypto startup that wants to save the journalism industry by leveraging the blockchain and crypto-economic.

It has partnered with the 172-year-old Associated Press to help the wire service stop bad actors from stealing its content.[15]

The reach of blockchain technology will go beyond the media and financial sector.

---

[15] https://techcrunch.com/2018/08/28/civil-the-blockchain-journalism-startup-has-partnered-with-one-of-the-oldest-names-in-media/

Microsoft's cloud platform Azure has introduced a Blockchain proof-of-authority (PoA) algorithm on its Ethereum (ETH) based product.

Qravity, a project that facilitates the production and distribution of digital entertainment, has launched a demo version of its platform[16], which enables decentralized creative teams to collaborate on content production and earn royalties for their work.

Their white paper [17] describes how Qravity will "provide a space for creative visionaries to collectively develop monetizable digital content" such as films, video games, music and other media. It is not hackable and can be trusted.

Transformative technologies are already being deployed as a substitute for trust.

The message is that if you can't trust a messenger, get a Blockchain.

In PR we are told that there is an important first step in any PR plan. It is to 'analyse the landscape in which the client exists'.

A lot of this information is available as data and content available to the public and the client. It comes from many sources including history books, press clippings and internet search, local authority records, the background about the client and its management, employees, vendors

---

16
https://l.facebook.com/l.php?u=https%3A%2F%2Fdemo.qravity.com%2Ffind-a-project&h=AT1ZZYLOD mG0EELhl6nQs_sPedNqPwJTHjpslZvy3Ozsbpk9S6xDCokaEAY-mO368PY4_I7AfAgCYi4-PrR7RrYrEU kCETd_KbSMaAJcYnq02zj8tS1L-20BKAuLkCz7x2Boc-RW

17 https://qravity.com/en/whitepaper/

and much much more. These data are fluid, the environment is changing all the time.

Surely no computer can assimilate so many factors such that it can be asked for insights into strengths and weaknesses and the extent to which an observation can be trusted.

But there is computing intelligence that has been designed to 'landscape' and provide patterns that can influence decisions.

The driverless car has such software.

It will need a lot of adaptation but is shows the extent to which technologies can be used even in the most complex environment and the prize is an ability to map the extent to which partners can be trusted.

Its fast, accurate and can be 'trusted'.

It is not that software is not usurping corporate decision making. There are examples that can be examined today:

Michael Schrage writing in Harvard Business Review in 2017 reported that:

"At some of the world's most successful enterprises — Google, Netflix, Amazon, Alibaba, Facebook — autonomous algorithms, not talented managers, increasingly get the last word. Elite MBAs (Management by Algorithm) are the new normal.

"Executives dedicated to data-driven excellence accept the reality that smart algorithms need greater autonomy to succeed. Empowering algorithms is now as organizationally important as empowering people.

"But without clear lines of authority and accountability, dual empowerment guarantees perpetual conflict between human and artificial intelligence."

Computational autonomy requires that C-suites revisit the hows and whys of delegation. "CEOs need to clarify when talented humans must defer to algorithmic judgment. That's hard. The most painful board conversations that I hear about machine learning revolve around how much power and authority super-smart software should have.

"Executives who wouldn't hesitate to automate a factory now flinch at the prospect of deep-learning algorithms dictating their sales strategies and capex. The implications of success scare them more than the risk of failure.

"Does this mean that all our procurement bids will be determined by machine?" asked one incredulous CEO of a multibillion euro business unit.

"Yes, that's exactly what it meant. His group's data science, procurement, and supply chain teams crafted algorithmic ensembles that, by all measures and simulations, would save hundreds of millions. Even better, they would respond 10 times faster to market moves than existing processes while requiring minimal human intervention. Top management would have to trust its computationally brilliant bidding software. That was the challenge. But the CEO wouldn't — or couldn't — pull the autonomy trigger.[18]"

---

18 https://hbr.org/2017/01/4-models-for-using-ai-to-make-decisions

In such an environment can the Corporate Affairs director not have the support of such machines or is she going to try and play the 20th century 'no comment' card?

8 HACKING TRUST IS A PR ISSUE

The other side of the coin is where technologies are used to damage trust.

Spam messages account for 48.16 percent of e-mail traffic worldwide. I guess that means we trust our spam filters and is an example of how we can easily take for granted defences already in place.

In the e-commerce industry alone, there are hundreds of thousands of sites in operation. All of these sites can benefit from investing in cybersecurity. Transactions conducted on e-commerce sites require the exchange of confidential data that can be compromised at any time if companies don't have the right type of cybersecurity protection.

And it's not just e-commerce companies that need to be wary of cyber thieves. Sensitive data like social security numbers, routing numbers, passcodes and other types of relevant information can be stolen for identity theft.

More than £2bn has been snatched from about one in 10 British adults, new data from Compare the Market has revealed, and online payments are the weakest link.

More than a quarter of frauds took place online last year and 27 per cent of victims don't know or remember how they were hacked.

The EU's General Data Protection Regulation (GDPR) has forced many of them to improve their data protection practices, but high-profile breaches are still occurring.

If a company's data is compromised and hackers get ahold of customers' credit card information, the company is responsible for that breach of data. What's even worse is that it has now lost the trust of loyal customers, losing a lot of revenue in recurring and potential new sales.

British Airways is an example. On 7th of September 2018, airline stocks were lower in late afternoon trade, with EasyJet down 1.2% to 1,444p and Ryanair Holdings down 1.7% at €13.33 and International Consolidated Airlines GroupSA (parent company to BA) shares off 3.2% to 659p after

British Airways said personal and financial details of hundreds of thousands of customers were stolen in a hack of its website and mobile app. Trust in BA took a knock and it showed in the share price.

The most common types of cyber attacks typically come from viruses, spam and identity fraud.

The rate at which such attack are reported is asstonishing. We tend to hear about t likes of BA, Reddit, Nexus and Samsung all in one week but that disguises the host of smaller organisations that have been compromised in the same few days. This is a big trust issue.

In addition, online bad mouthing and threats to organisations and individual are also significant because they affect reputation whether guilty or not.

Here again we see transformative technologies coming to aid the Professional PR person.

Up front is the monitoring service used to monitor organisation security breaches, social media and comments left on websites which also applies to employees and key publics and cultures.

There are established patterns that pressage many such attacks notably in the structure of key online networks. Later in the cycles evidence of 'rubbernecking' . This is when people use the internet to verify rumour or to keep up to date with events. This is manifest, for example, in spikes of interest evident in search engines. This reputation monitoring is important to allow issues and crisis management programmes to be implemented (see the *Crisis and Transformative Technologies* essay in this series on Amazon). A well managed issue of crisis can be a big downer or can enhance trust in people and organisations.

Because the Public Relations professional is the most likely person the manage online content, S/he is now catapulted into digital issues and crisis management. How good is the PR department internet monitoring? Is it limited to just social media? Is its monitoring enough to be a front line defence against attacks on the trustworthiness of the organisation?

The information security threat landscape is constantly evolving. The biggest threats are well known and they should all be included in organisation issues and crisis management planning. In addition all PR consultants should be in a position to advise or call on expertise for planning and management.

Top of the list is, strangely, fragile connectivity. Organisations depend of instant and uninterrupted connectivity, smart physical devices and trustworthy people. But that dependence makes them vulnerable to attacks on core internet infrastructure, devices used in daily business and key people with access to mission-critical information. If the network or WiFi dies, the prospects for maintaining stakeholder trust is compromised. It is seen as a sign of poor management capability.

Organisations need to rethink their defensive models, particularly regarding business continuity and disaster recovery plans. Plans that rely on employees working from home won't survive attacks that remove connectivity or that target key individuals.

As conflicts across the globe increase in number and severity, some predict that within the next few years, nation states and other groups will seek new ways of causing widespread disruption, including internet outages at the local or even regional level. In the UK the National Health Service (with 1.4 million employees!) has already been compromised by such an attack.

Given the increasing prevalence of 'just-in-time' supply chain models, even brief disruptions can lead to shortages.

Banks and financial institutions are at risk too.

Attacks of this kind could involve physically cutting cables (possibly under sea where repairs could take significant time), rendering root DNS or datacenters useless, distributed denial of service (DDos) attacks that harness massive botnets or even manipulating internet addresses and routes to ensure traffic doesn't arrive at its stated destination.

Individuals and organisations now have to understand the extent of their reliance on the internet and have plans in place to address the risk of attacks that recur on a relatively frequent basis.

Criminals are increasingly profiting from ransomware — encrypting a victim's data and then demanding payment for the encryption key. The U.S. Federal Bureau of Investigation (FBI) estimated last year that cybercriminals would generate about $1 billion in revenue from ransomware by the end of 2016. A global cyberattack using hacking tools widely believed by researchers to have been developed by the US National Security Agency crippled the NHS, hit international shipper FedEx and infected computers in 150 countries.

Cybercriminals will increasingly focus their ransomware efforts on smart devices connected to the Internet of Things (IoT). Attackers may hold specific devices for ransom, but they will also use the devices as gateways to install ransomware on other devices and systems throughout organisations.

Embedded technologies are now becoming commonplace and need to be included in the crisis contingency planning of the Public Relations professional.

Business may be high-tech and digital, but employees exist in the physical world, and that makes them vulnerable to blackmail, intimidation and violence. These privileged insiders may be senior business managers and highly placed executives, but they could also be their personal assistants, systems administrators, infrastructure architects, network support engineers and even specific external contractors.

A contingency plan might include identifying mission-critical information assets and the individuals who own and access them. Implementation of mechanisms to protect the organisation against the insider threat. (e.g., screen prospective employees; embedding appropriate clauses in employment contracts). Maybe adopt a trust-but-verify approach to privileged insiders (e.g., foster a culture of trust, while verifying and monitoring appropriate system access).

Business depend upon accurate and reliable information. If the integrity of that information is compromised, so is the business. In the past it has been assumed this is an IT security matter, but it's more akin to risk management in the information space.

Organisations can reduce the effect of misinformation by monitoring what others say about the organisation online and keeping track of changes made to internal information to provide early warning signals.

Advances in artificial intelligence allows for the creation of chatbots that will soon be indistinguishable from humans. Attackers will be (are) able to use these chatbots to spread misinformation. Without ever breaching an organization's digital boundary an attacker could damage that its reputation by spreading convincing misinformation about its working practices or products. A single attacker could deploy hundreds of chatbots, each spreading malicious information and rumors over social media and news sites.

Attacks won't just target reputation. Fake news can also be used to manipulate a company's share price. German payments company Wirecard AG found that out the hard way. In 2017 a fake report 'detailed' fraudulent activities by the company. While the report was later proven fake, the company's share price plummeted and took three months to recover.

9 Conclusion

Trust is essential and is a basic in PR. It has to be treated differently to reputation. It is a well-researched area of humankind. It is commercially important and has considerable commercial value.

There is much that a PR practitioner might consider in dealing with issues of trust as part of the job of PR, but now there are a number of new considerations that need to be thought through as technologies begin to come centre stage.

When reputation is damaged it has an effect on perceptions of trust but when trust is undermined reputation is much more fundamentally compromised.

On the other hand, the evolving technologies offer very powerful means for monitoring and affecting the perceptions of trust and thereby reputation.

Perhaps now is an opportunity to consider the evolving technologies that are going to offer you yet another opportunity to to developm the professional career. in PR.

The evolution of technologies that can acquire big data, facilities to store and analyse it and software to build trust models for commercial use is now available.

This is an area of fast developments and an opportunity to implement additional research is wide open.

David Phillips
September 2018

9 ENDNOTE

This is quite a long essay and yet there is so much more to tell. I am sure that many colleagues and students will want to challenge my views and comment on what is here.

I welcome such debate and am not in the least fragile about criticism.

David

www.ingramcontent.com/pod-product-compliance
Lightning Source LLC
Chambersburg PA
CBHW071441220526
45469CB00004B/1619